MW01153342

ISBN-13: 978-0615725642
ISBN-10: 0615725643

Dingding, Ningning, Singsing and other fun Tagalog words

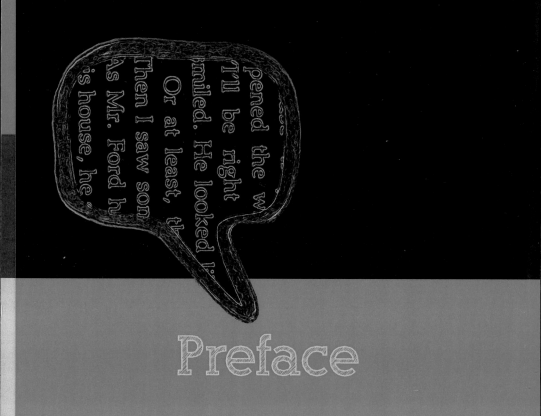

Preface

"Too-big please" say my husband, Tony, and our five year old son, Emil. "*Tubig*" means water in Tagalog.

I was born in Manila, where Tagalog is widely spoken, and moved to the US for grad school. My Nebraska-born husband and I met at New York University and decided to settle in New York City. When our son, Emil, w bor012 born, we decided that I would teach him Tagalog.

Because my husband did not know the language, it was hard for me to sustain my devotion to teaching it. I discovered, however, that for both Emil and my husband, the fun sounding words were easy to remember and enjoyable to learn.

I wrote this book for English-speaking families of Filipino descent like ours. I have added the word in phonogram form to help with pronunciation and my good friend, Lizza Y. Gutierrez, designed the book and created the ingenious illustrations. We hope this book will be a fun way to introduce the language and culture of the Philippines.

There are many fun sounding Tagalog words. I used the following criteria to select the words in this book:

- Repetitions
    - For example: *dingding* (wall), *ningning* (sparkle), and *singsing* (ring)

- Everyday words used by families with young children
    - For example: *kiliti* (tickle), *tigil* (stop), *busog* (full), and *tulog* (sleep)

- Names of bugs
    - Many children I know are fascinated by bugs and coincidentally, Tagalog words for bugs sound funny to many English speakers. For example: *tutubi* (dragonfly), and *tipaklong* (grasshopper).

- Words used in Tagalog children's songs and lullabies
    - For example: *talong* (eggplant) and *buko* (coconut) appear in the folk songs "*Bahay Kubo*" and "*Leron Leron Sinta.*"

"*Gigil*" is special. "*Gigil*" means having so much of a (happy, angry, excited, or frustrated) feeling inside that it just has to be expressed. It's a feeling that children often have and for some grown ups like me— who still wear their hearts on their sleeves—one that is not outgrown.

Sound Clues:

at

navy

end

me

big

silent

odd

open

do

up

music

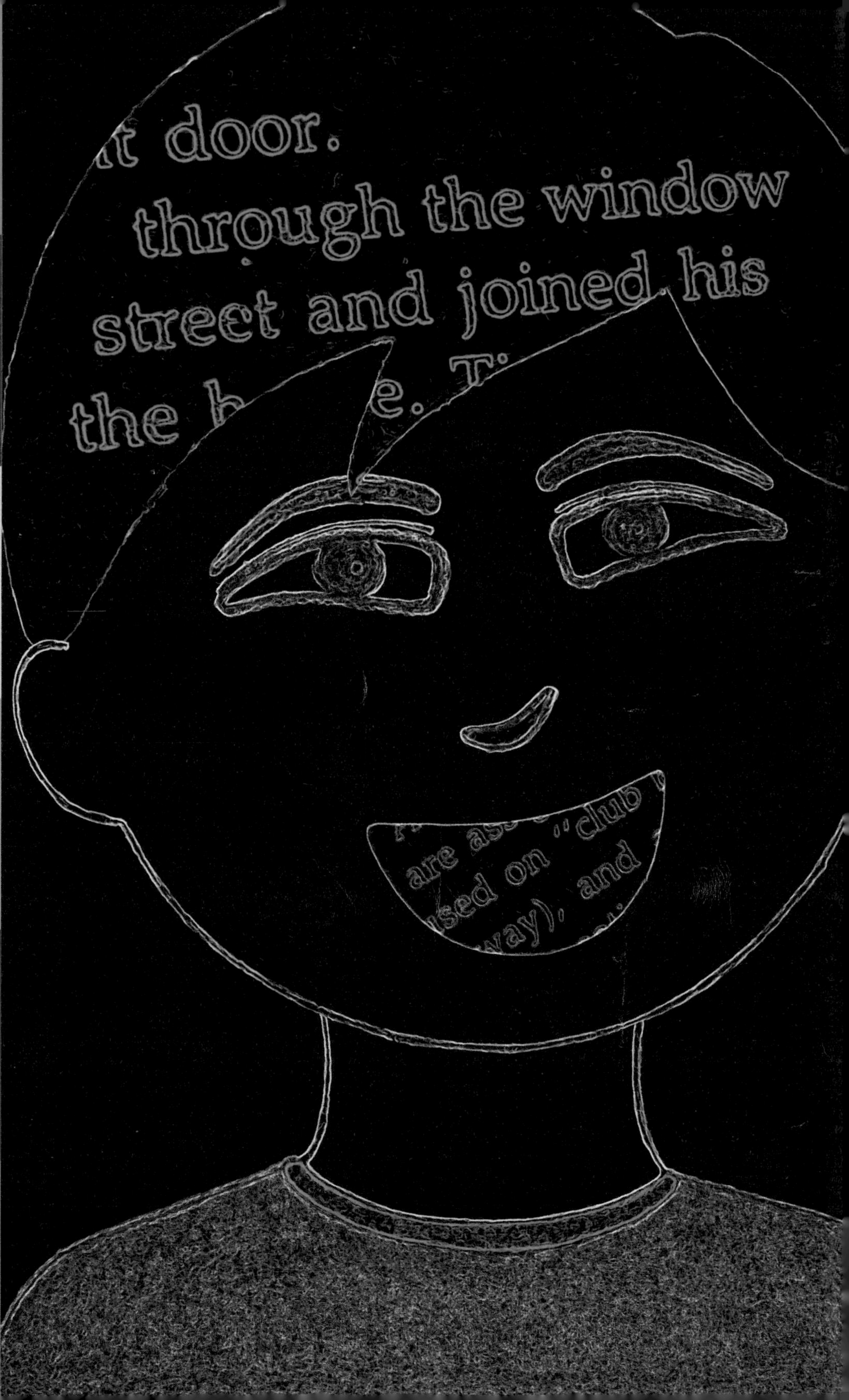

Hi, my name is Emil.

My mom is from the Philippines
and she is teaching me Tagalog.

There are many fun sounding words like

dingding, *ningning*, and *singsing*.

Would you like to learn them with me?

Meaning : A wall of lightweight material
like the walls in a playhouse
or *bahay kubo*.

In Tagalog: *Isinabit ni Nanay ang iginuhit
ko sa **dingding** ng aming kubo.*

In English : Mama hung my drawing on
the wall of our hut.

SOUND CLUE: dǐngdǐng

Ningning

Meaning   :   The twinkling of stars.

In Tagalog: *Kagabi, pinagmasdan namin*
               ang ningning ng mga bituin.

In English :   Last night, we watched the
                twinkling of stars.

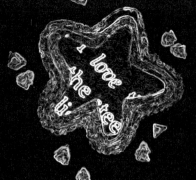

SOUND CLUE: nǐngnǐng

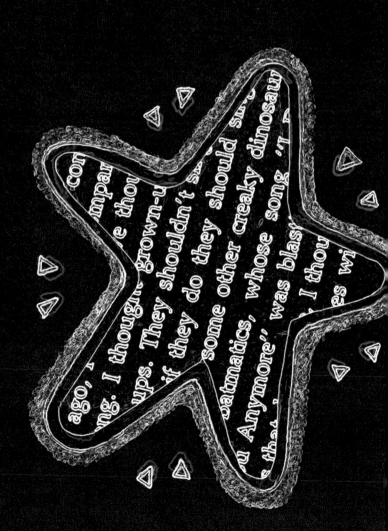

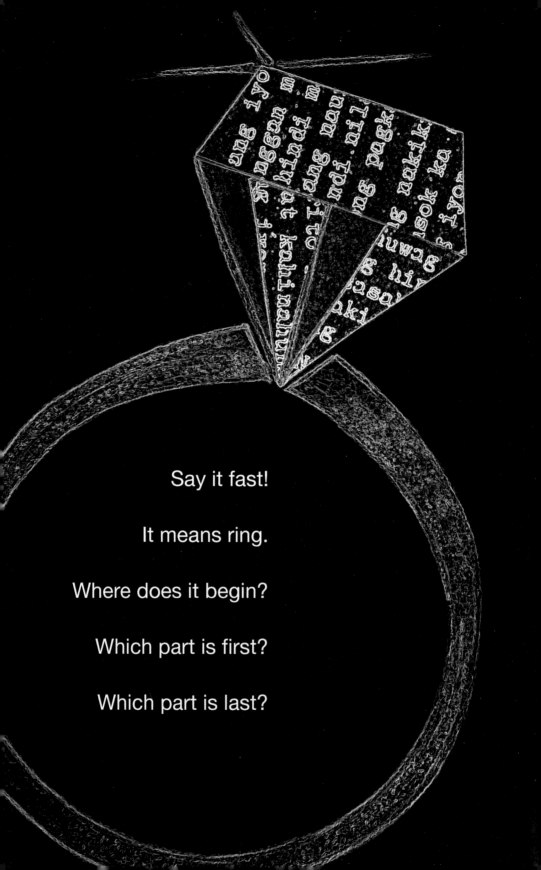

Say it fast!

It means ring.

Where does it begin?

Which part is first?

Which part is last?

Singsing!

SOUND CLUE: sĭngsĭng

"*Oo*" means yes.

Say "oh-o," not "uh-oh."

"Would you like some juice?," my Mama asks.

"*Oo*," I say.

Or "*opo*," the formal way.

SOUND CLUE: ŏŏ

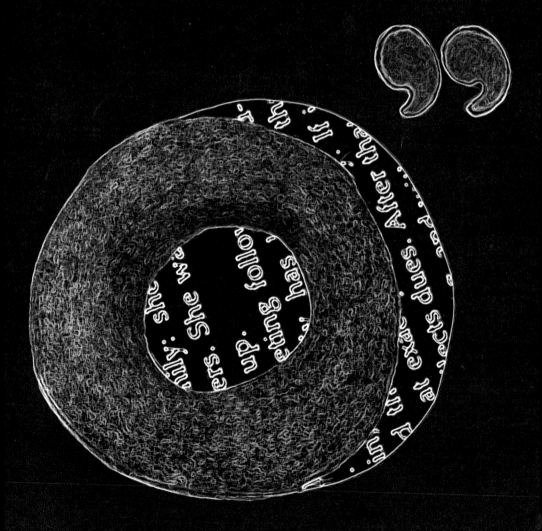

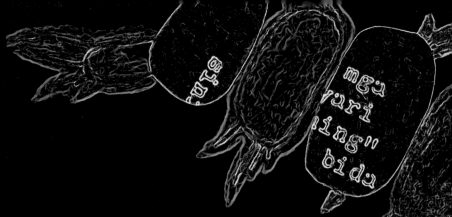

Meaning   :   Mosquito larvae. (In the
                Philippines, wiggly children
                are called *kitikiti*.)

In Tagalog: *Kapag nasa simbahan kami,
              sabi ni Nanay na huwag kang
              parang **kitikiti**.*

In English :   When we are at church, Mama
               says, "Try not to wiggle so much
               like the baby mosquitoes."

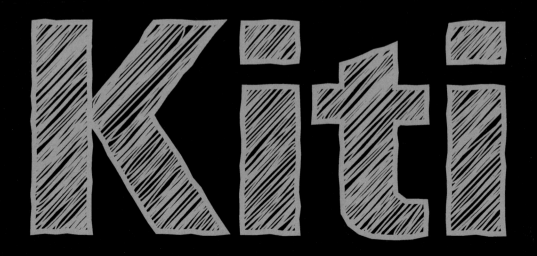

Kiti

kĭtĭ

ikili

Say "*kilikili*!" *Kilikili*!

It means underarms.

I love tickling my Papa's *kilikili*.

We love being silly.

Meaning   :   Place on your body where you are ticklish.

In Tagalog: *Nasa talampakan ang kiliti ng kaibigan kong si Nicholas.*

In English :   My friend, Nicholas, is ticklish in the feet.

SOUND CLUE: kĭlētē

Meaning : Having so much of a feeling
(happy, angry, excited, frustrated)
inside you that you have to let it
out by scrunching your face,
squeezing your hands into a fist,
or pinching the person next
to you.

In Tagalog: *Gigil na gigil ako kapag nakikita
ko si Ms. Zayda, ang aking
paboritong guro!*

In English : I want to squeeze Ms. Zayda
when I see her. She is my
favorite teacher!

Gigil

SOUND CLUE: gĭgĭl

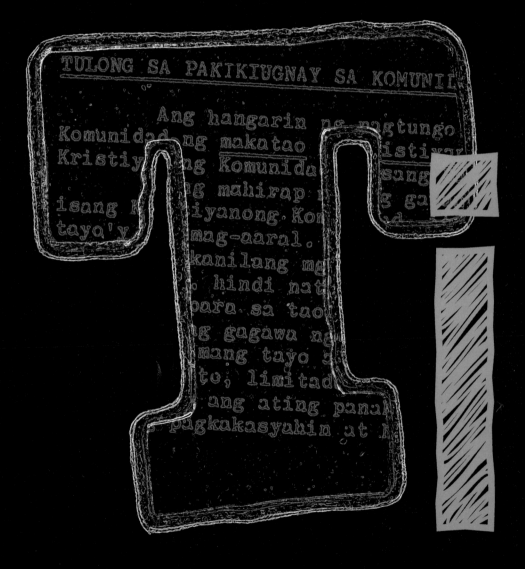

TULONG SA PAKIKIUGNAY SA KOMUNID

Ang hangarin ng pagtungo
Komunidad ng makatao   istiya
Kristiyanong Komunida   sang
isang Kristiyanong Kon   g ga
tayo'y   mag-aaral.
              kanilang ma
           hindi na
        para sa tao
      g gagawa ng
      mang tayo
      to; limitad
      ang ating panah
      pagkakasyahin at

SOUND CLUE: tigil

Meaning   :   Stop

In Tagalog: *"Tigil na sa paglaro!,"* sabi ni
Nanay. Oras na para kumain.

In English :   "Stop playing now!" said Mama.
It is time to eat.

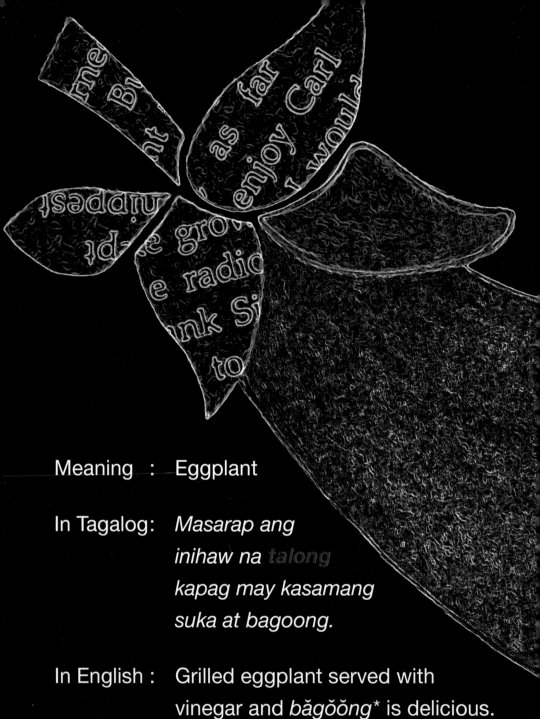

Meaning : Eggplant

In Tagalog: *Masarap ang
inihaw na talong
kapag may kasamang
suka at bagoong.*

In English : Grilled eggplant served with
vinegar and *băgŏŏng** is delicious.

Băgŏŏng is a condiment widely used in the Philippines. It is made
with tiny fish or shrimp and flavored with salt, garlic, and onions. Yum!

Talong

SOUND CLUE: tălŏng

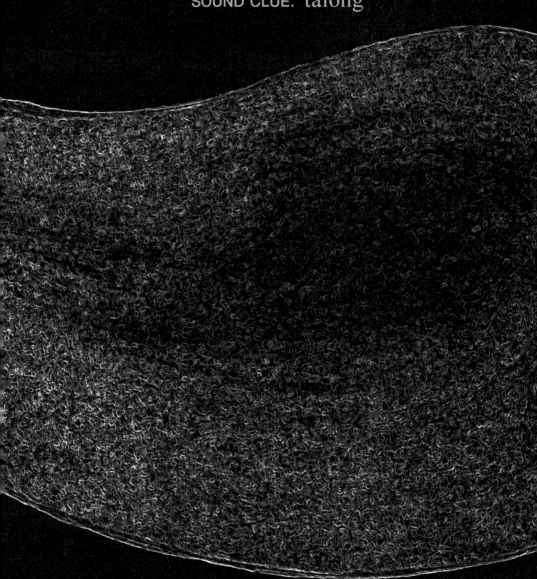

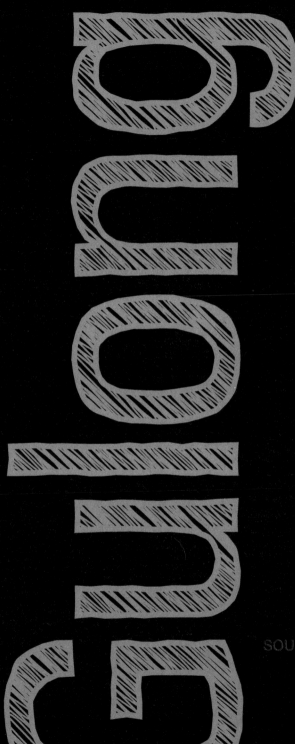

SOUND CLUE: gōōlŏng

Meaning : Wheel

In Tagalog: *Tinulungan ko si Tatay sa pagpalit ng gulong ng aming kotse.*

In English : I helped Papa change the tire of our car.

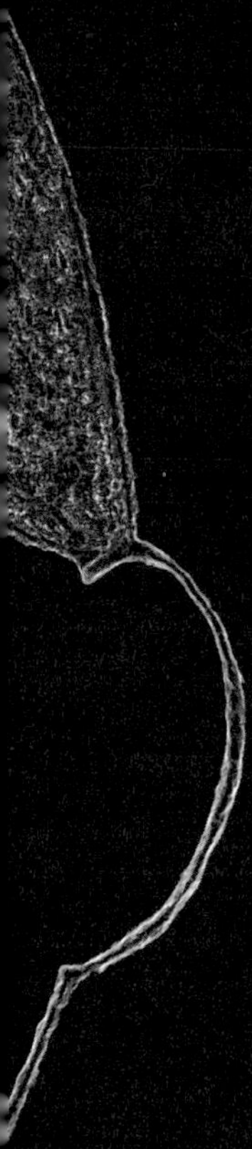

Say "eee-long."

It means nose.

When I was a baby, my *Lolo* (grandfather)

would play a game in which he bounced

my legs and touched my *ilong* with my toes.

Ilong

SOUND CLUE: ēlŏng

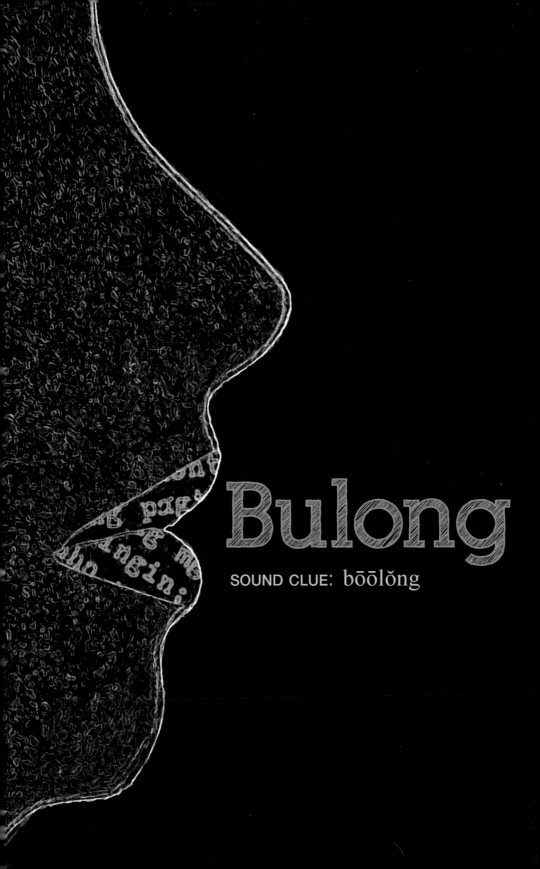

Bulong

SOUND CLUE: bōōlŏng

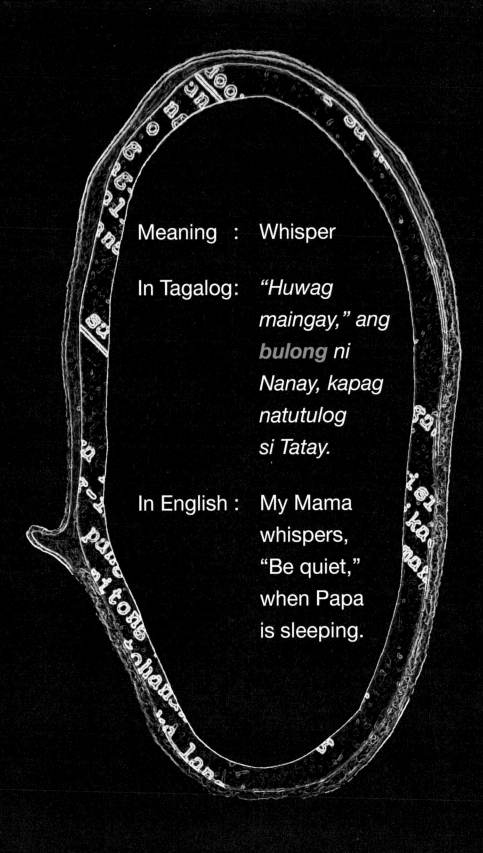

Meaning : Whisper

In Tagalog: *"Huwag maingay," ang **bulong** ni Nanay, kapag natutulog si Tatay.*

In English : My Mama whispers, "Be quiet," when Papa is sleeping.

Meaning : Coconut

In Tagalog: *Nakatikim ka na ba ng buko*
ice cream? Ang sarap!

In English : Have you ever tried coconut
ice cream? It's delicious!

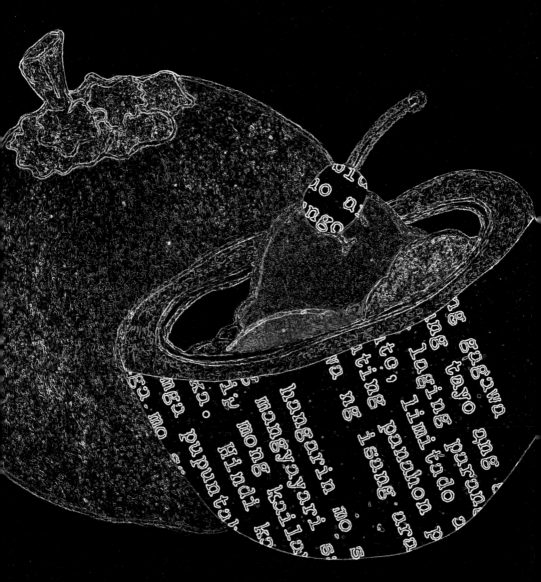

SOUND CLUE: bōōkǒ

SOUND CLUE: bōōsŏg

Meaning   :   Full

In Tagalog: *Ayoko nang kumain, busog*
              na busog na ako.

In English :   I don't want to eat any more.
               I am so full.

Bubuyog

Meaning : Bee

In Tagalog: *Noong nakaraang tag-araw, nakahuli ako ng **bubuyog**. Pero kinagat niya ako!*

In English : Last summer, I caught a bee. But I was stung!

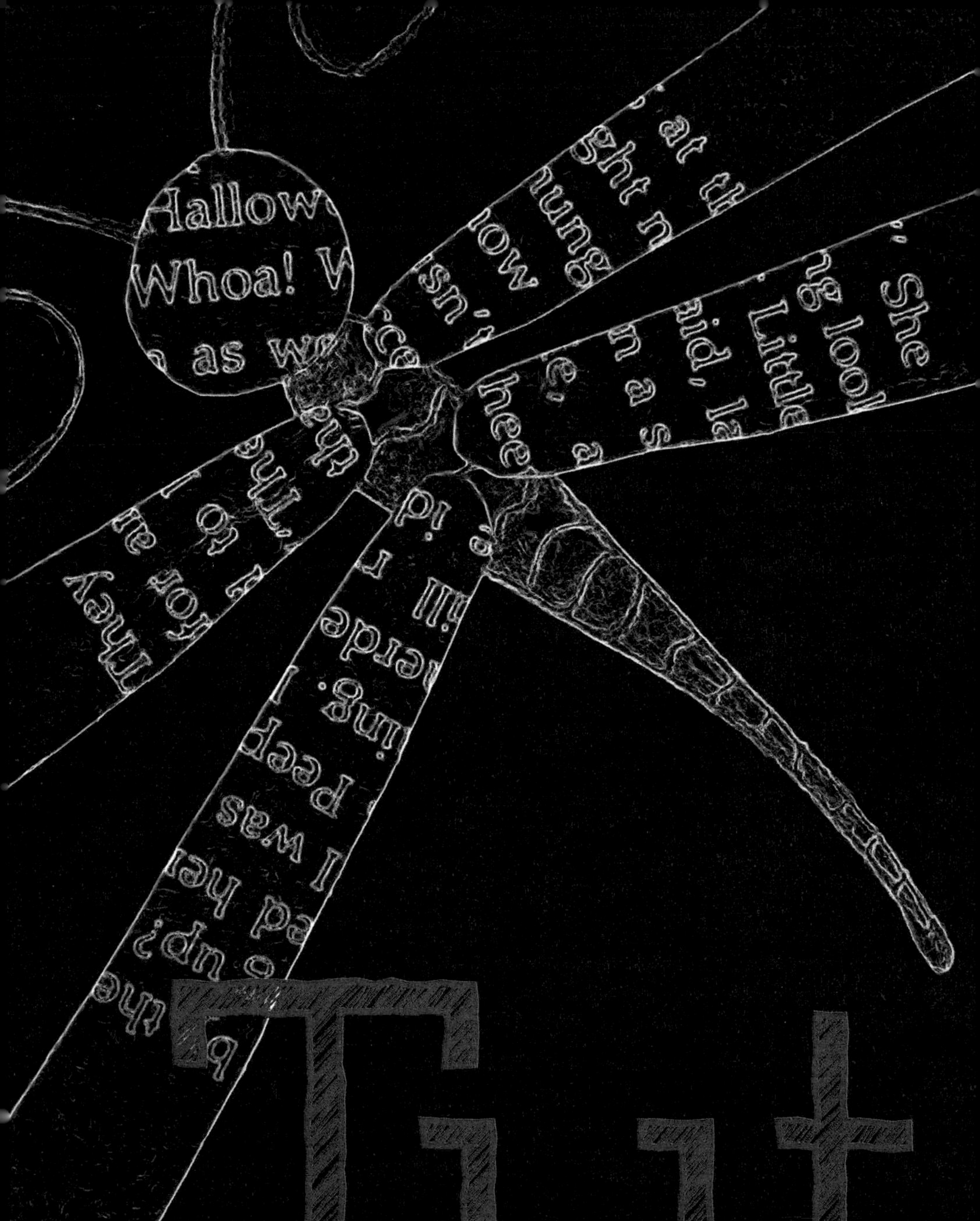

Tut

Say "2-2-bee."

"*Tutubi*" means dragonfly.

Do you know that instead of two,
they have thousands of little eyes?

The eyes tell them I am near.

They need all those eyes since they
don't have ears.

SOUND CLUE: părūpărŏ

Paru

paro

Meaning : Butterfly

In Tagalog: *Nabasa namin ni Nanay na nakasara ang pakpak ng **paruparo** kapag ito'y nagpapahinga.*

In English : Mama and I read that butterflies rest with their wings close together.

Meaning   :   Moth

In Tagalog: *Ang gamugamo naman ay*
nagpapahinga na nakabuka
ang pakpak.

In English :   Moths rest with wings
set apart.

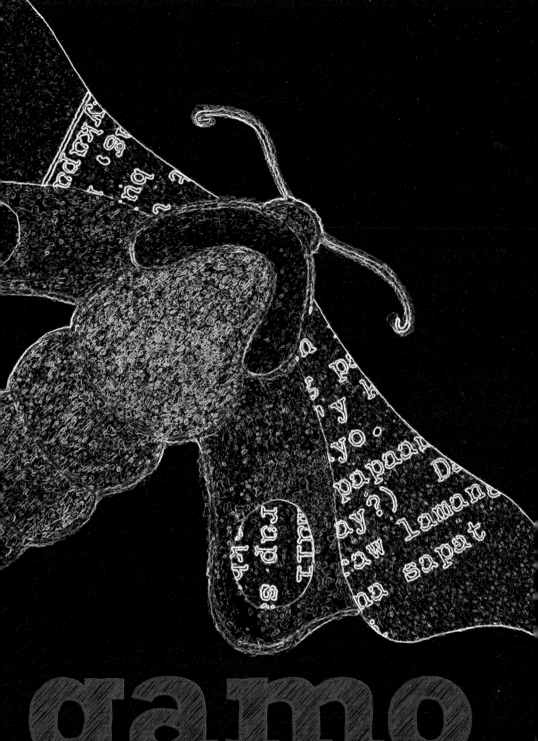

gamo

SOUND CLUE: gămūgămŏ

SOUND CLUE: tēpăklŏng

Meaning : Grasshopper

In Tagalog: *Nakakita kami ng mga kalaro ko ng isang berdeng tipaklong sa liwasan.*

In English : My friends and I saw a bright green grasshopper at the park.

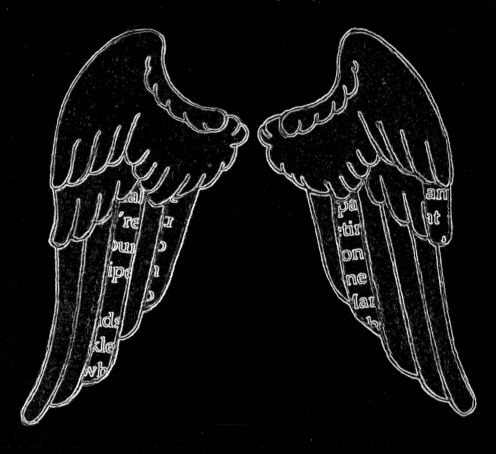

Meaning   :   Wings

In Tagalog: *Nais kong magkaroon ng*
                     mga **pakpak***, para madali*
                     akong makatago tulad
                     ng mga insekto.

In English :   I wish I had wings so I
                     could easily hide just like
                     the bugs.

wan

Pak-one, pak-two, pak-three, pak-four.

"Pakwan" means watermelon.

My favorite fruit! May I have some more?

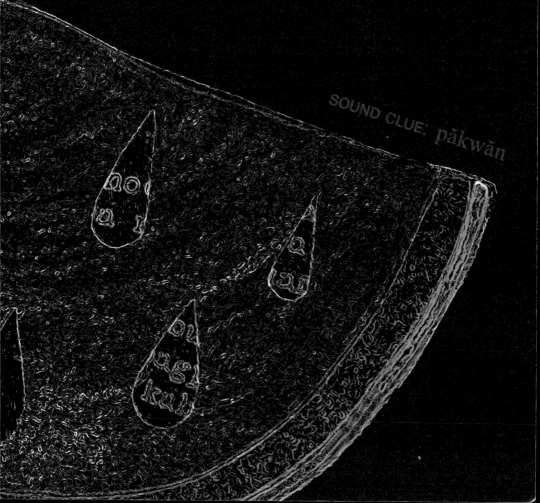

SOUND CLUE: păkwăn

SOUND CLUE: tōōgtŏg

Meaning : Music

In Tagalog: *Mahilig kami ni Tatay na sumayaw sa **tugtog**.*

In English : Papa and I like to dance to music.

Tugtog

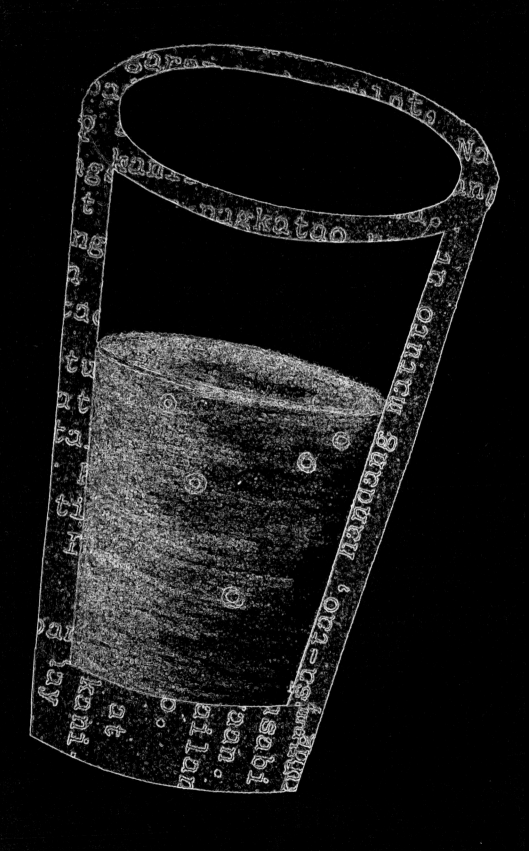

Meaning : Water

In Tagalog: *Pahingi po* ng **tubig**?*

In English : May I have some water, please?

SOUND CLUE: tōō-bǐg

*Filipinos use *"po"* when talking
to someone who is older.

Say "too-log."

"*Tulog*" means sleep.

Papa says I need my *tulog*

but sometimes I peep.

SOUND CLUE: to͞olŏg

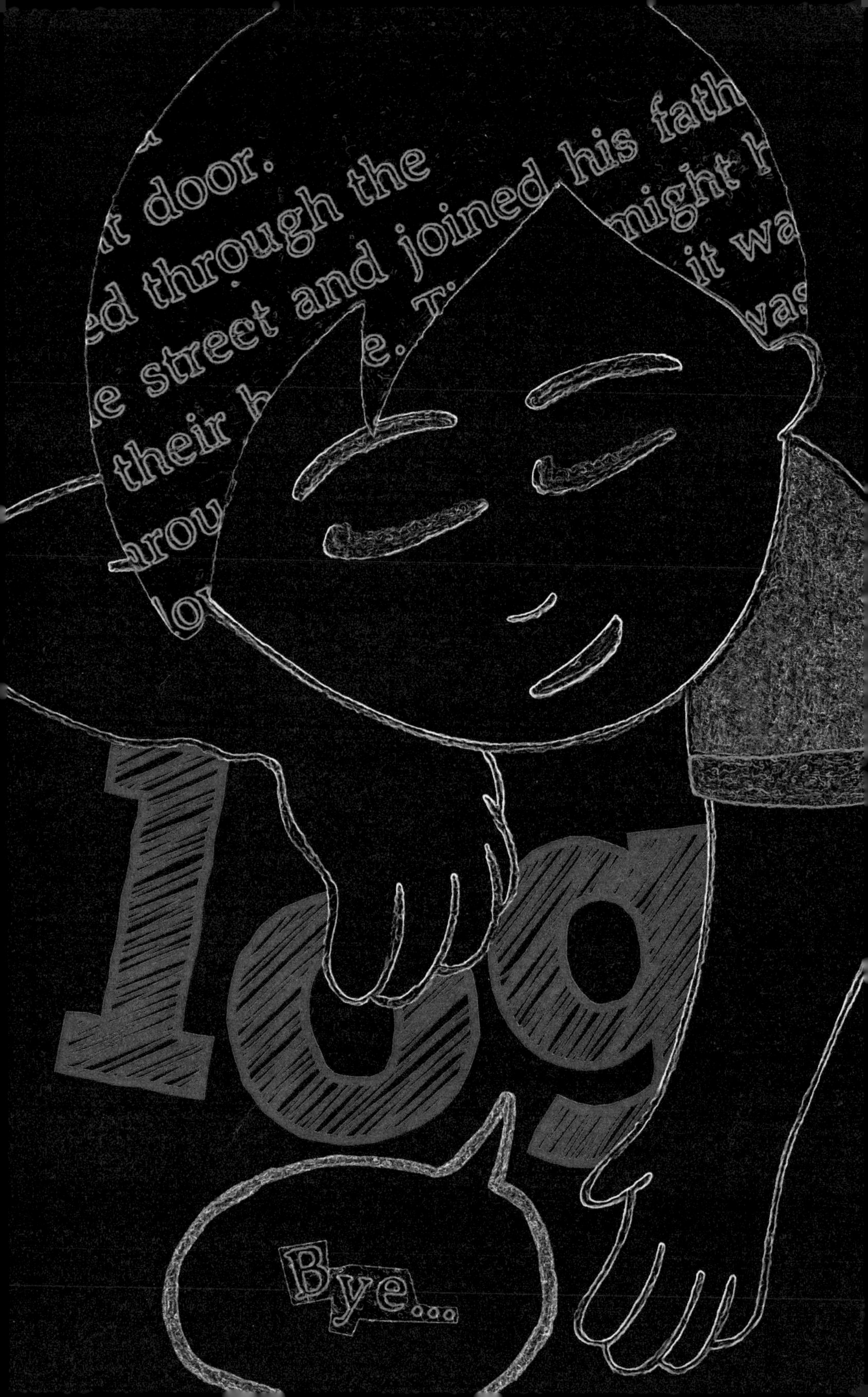

Bahay Kubo

Bahay kubo, kahit munti
Ang halaman doon, ay sari sari
Sinkamas at talong, sigarilyas at mani
Sitaw, bataw, patani!
Kundol, patola, upo't kalabasa
At saka mayroon pang labanos, mustasa,
Sibuyas, kamatis, bawang at luya
Sa paligid-ligid ay puno ng linga.

Some Tagalog Folk Songs

Nipa Hut

My nipa hut although it is small

Has many plants that grow very tall

Turnips and eggplants, winged beans and peanuts

String beans, hyacinth beans, and lima beans!

Wax gourds, sponge gourds, white squash

and pumpkins,

And there is more: Radish, mustard,

onions, tomatoes, garlic, and ginger

And all around are sesame seeds.

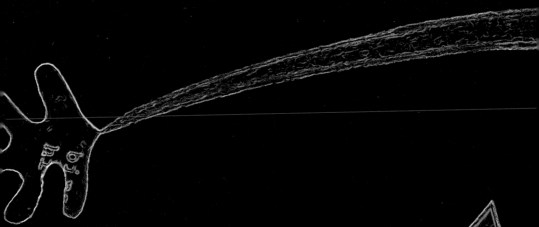

Leron, Leron, Sinta

Leron, leron sinta
Buko ng papaya,
Dala-dala'y buslo,
Sisidlan ng sinta,
Pagdating sa dulo'y
Nabali ang sanga
Kapos kapalaran,
Humanap ng iba.

Gumising ka, Neneng,
Tayo'y manampalok,
Dalhin mo ang buslo
Sisidlan ng hinog.
Pagdating sa dulo'y
Lalamba-lambayog,
Kumapit ka, Neneng,
Baka ka mahulog.

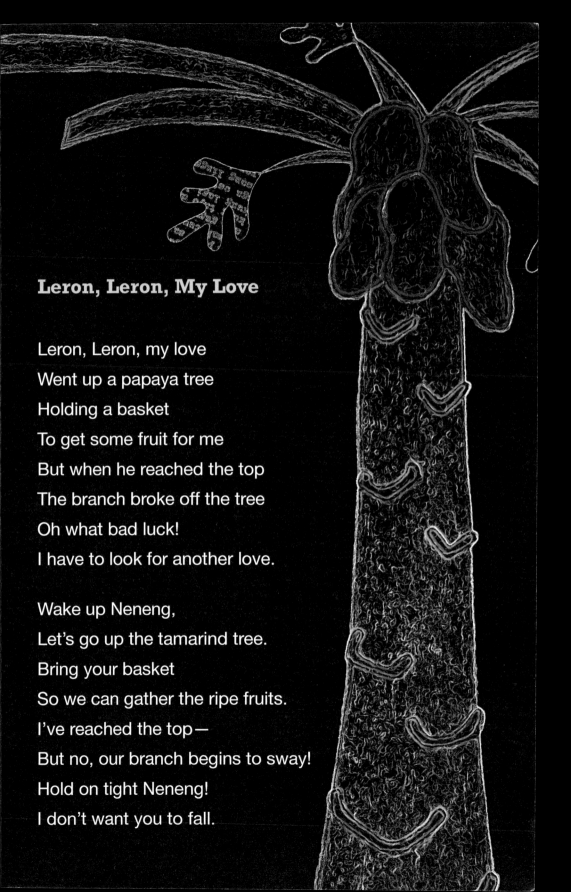

Leron, Leron, My Love

Leron, Leron, my love
Went up a papaya tree
Holding a basket
To get some fruit for me
But when he reached the top
The branch broke off the tree
Oh what bad luck!
I have to look for another love.

Wake up Neneng,
Let's go up the tamarind tree.
Bring your basket
So we can gather the ripe fruits.
I've reached the top—
But no, our branch begins to sway!
Hold on tight Neneng!
I don't want you to fall.

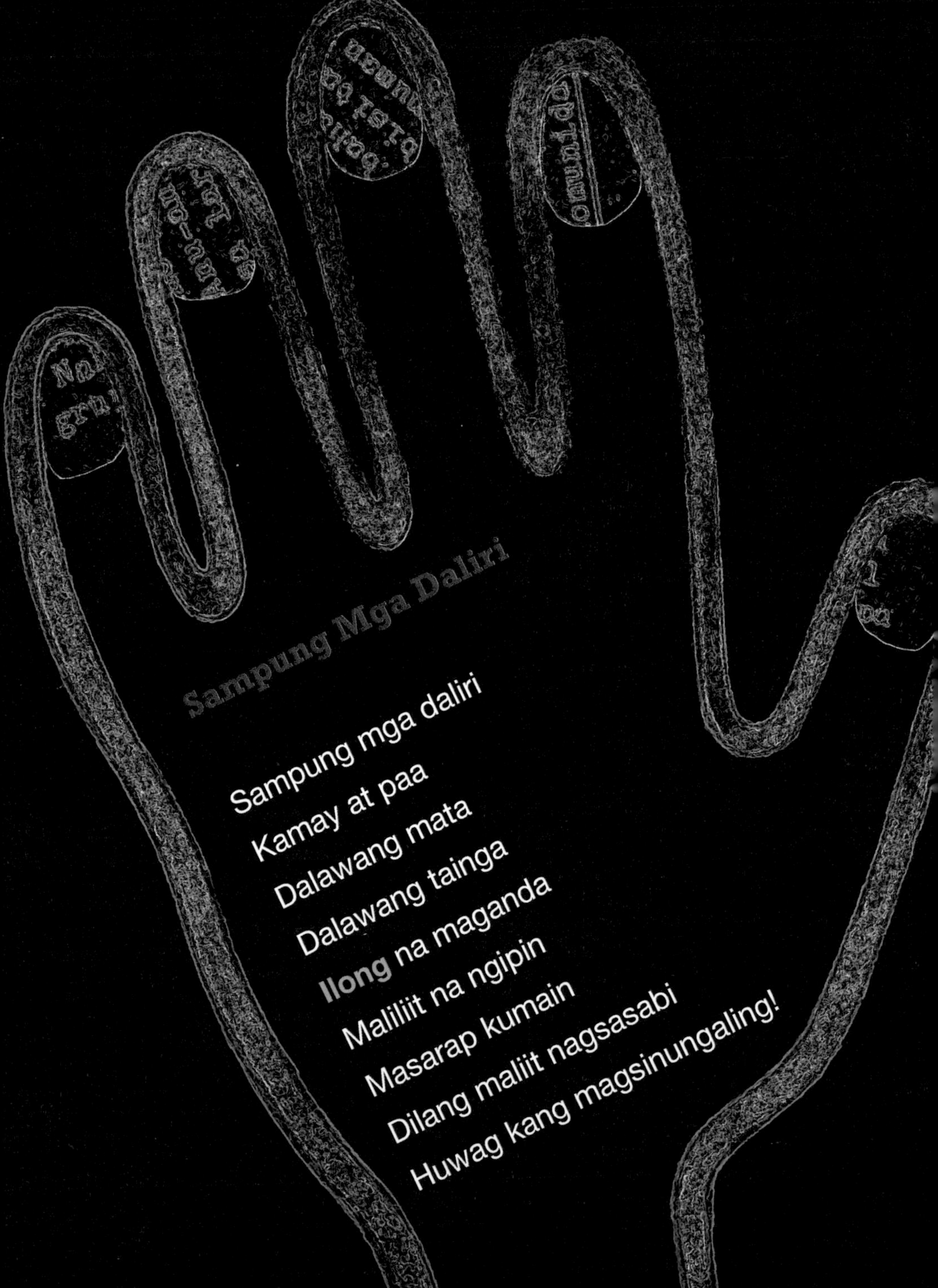

Sampung Mga Daliri

Sampung mga daliri
Kamay at paa
Dalawang mata
Dalawang tainga
Ilong na maganda
Maliliit na ngipin
Masarap kumain
Dilang maliit nagsasabi
Huwag kang magsinungaling!

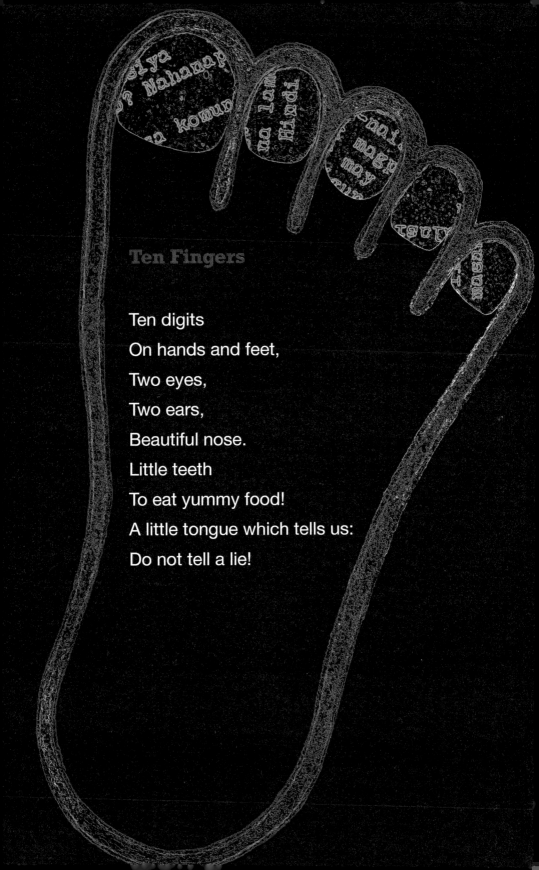

Ten Fingers

Ten digits

On hands and feet,

Two eyes,

Two ears,

Beautiful nose.

Little teeth

To eat yummy food!

A little tongue which tells us:

Do not tell a lie!

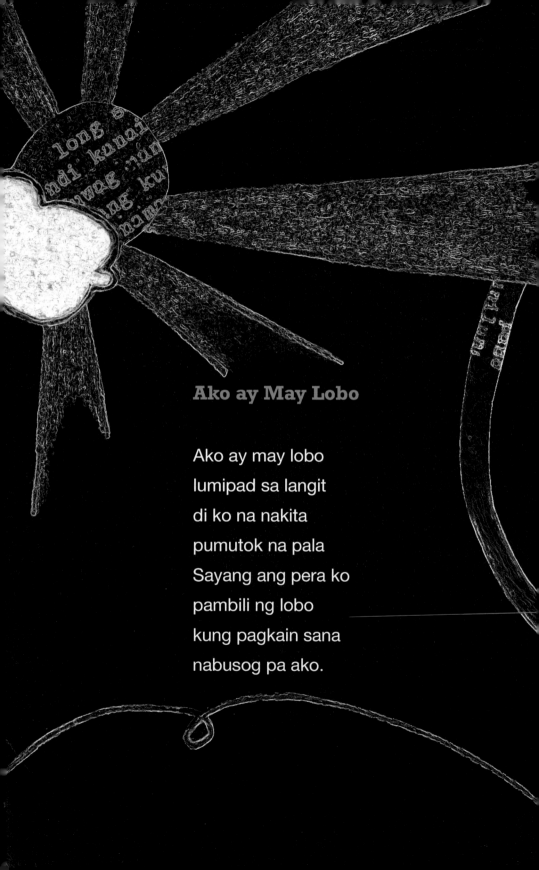

Ako ay May Lobo

Ako ay may lobo
lumipad sa langit
di ko na nakita
pumutok na pala
Sayang ang pera ko
pambili ng lobo
kung pagkain sana
nabusog pa ako.

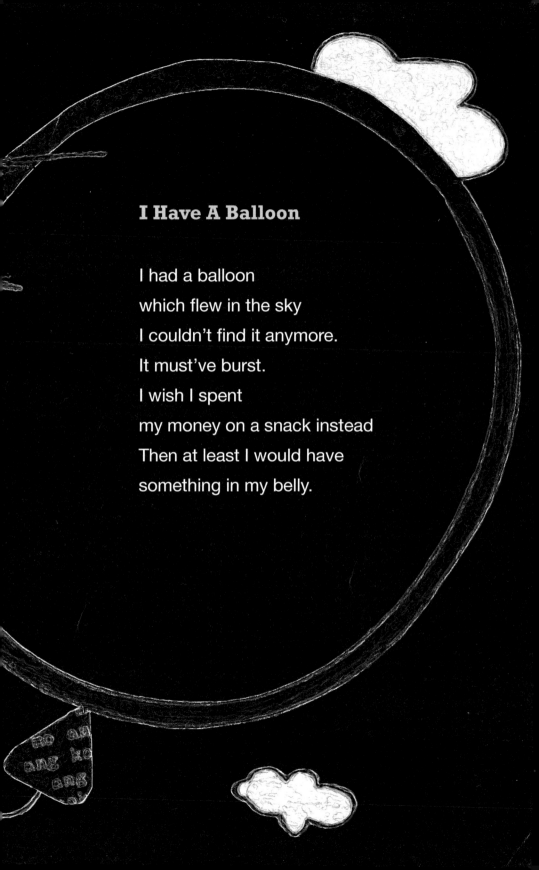

I Have A Balloon

I had a balloon
which flew in the sky
I couldn't find it anymore.
It must've burst.
I wish I spent
my money on a snack instead
Then at least I would have
something in my belly.

Sa Ugoy Ng Duyan

Sana'y di magmaliw ang dati kong araw

Nang munti pang bata sa piling ni Nanay

Nais kong maulit ang awit ni Inang mahal

Awit ng pag-ibig habang ako'y nasa duyan

Sa aking pagtulog na labis ang himbing

Ang bantay ko'y tala

Ang tanod ko'y bituin

Sa piling ni Nanay

Langit ang buhay

Puso kong may dusa

Sabik sa ugoy ng

duyan mo Inay

Sana narito ka Inay

To Be Rocked in my Cradle

I wish it would never end —
Those days when I was a little child in my mother's arms
I wish I could hear again my mama's lullabies
She would sing me love songs while I slept in my cradle
while I slept soundly,
the stars watched over me
the constellations looked out for me.
In my mother's arms,
I am in heaven.
My heart aches
I long to be in the cradle of my mother's arms
Mama, I wish you were here.

Can you think of other fun sounding words?
Draw a Picture!

Send your drawing and list to us, to post on our website, through
dingding@givebackmail.com

Visit our website: *www.dingdingningningsingsing.com*
Like us on Facebook: *www.facebook.com/DingdingNingningSingsing*

Make a List!

1. BUYKOS

2. BUYKOS

3. BUYKOS

4. BUYKOS

5. BUYKOS

...kabataan
.lapitan sila, dah...
.hanapin ang may ka...
-iwasan ang paglalako...
: maging suplado o
wag ring maging
sali sa kanilang maw...
kantahan, umaw...
-maging paminsan-mins...
-makinig paminsan rin ng
magbasa-basa rin ng
binong pinapanood
Malaki! gigibig!
daigdig!

We appreciate your supporting us and hope you had as much fun reading this book as we did writing and illustrating it.

Thank you to our friends and family:

Cynthia Arre
sr. bubbles bandojo, rc
Jun Jun and Esther Capistrano
Jeff Chou
Angeli Gutierrez
Noli and Ninot Gutierrez
Shiela Iiams
Teresita Jose
Emil Kelso
Tony Kelso
Cecille Capistrano-Poblador
Titchie and Erwin Tiongson
Riza Witzke

Acknowledgements

About the Author

TRICIA J. CAPISTRANO's essays have appeared in *Newsweek, MrBellersNeighborhood.com, The Philippine Star, ANI 32: The Global Pinoy Issue*, and *Hanggang Sa Muli, Homecoming Stories for the Filipino Soul*. She is also co-author of the blog pinoystudyabroad.blogspot.com. Tricia was born in Manila and moved to New York City in her early 20s. She now lives in Inwood, New York City, with her husband, Tony Kelso, and their son Emil. This is her first children's book.

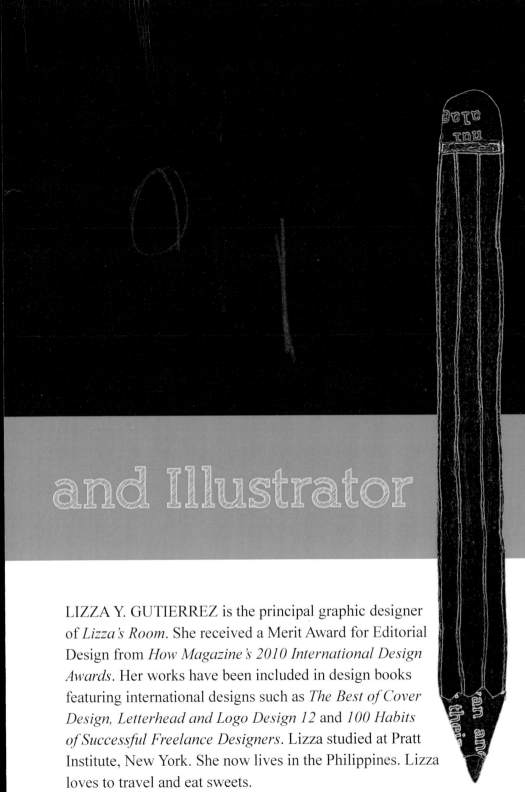

and Illustrator

LIZZA Y. GUTIERREZ is the principal graphic designer of *Lizza's Room*. She received a Merit Award for Editorial Design from *How Magazine's 2010 International Design Awards*. Her works have been included in design books featuring international designs such as *The Best of Cover Design, Letterhead and Logo Design 12* and *100 Habits of Successful Freelance Designers*. Lizza studied at Pratt Institute, New York. She now lives in the Philippines. Lizza loves to travel and eat sweets.